FRUI
ANI
VEGETABLE SALAD

Fresh and Colorful Recipes for Everyday

Mary Lopez

work can be in any fashion deemed liable for any hardship or damages that may befall them after undertaking information described herein.

Additionally, the information in the following pages is intended only for informational purposes and should thus be thought of as universal. As befitting its nature, it is presented without assurance regarding its prolonged validity or interim quality. Trademarks that are mentioned are done without written consent and can in no way be considered an endorsement from the trademark holder.

TABLE OF CONTENTS

Introduction

Salad: by itself this word means everything and it means nothing! Colorful and rich in taste, salads are the undisputed stars of the summer. No rules to follow, everything is allowed to make them appetizing and inviting. The avocado salad, for example, takes advantage of all the beneficial properties and the unique taste of this fresh and pulpy superfood, while the crispy chicken salad with vinaigrette transforms this dish into a genuine and substantial single dish.

The great thing about salads is that you just need to put together many different ingredients each time to create a different dish: never the usual salad, but always delicious dishes! Even a simple potato salad can become delicious if seasoned in the right way: it will surprise you!

Talking about salads means entering a vast, non-codable, and creative world. We can use all kinds of ingredients, although in international cuisine there are salads with a curious origin, which have rightfully entered the international gastronomy. Hated by children, but also by many adults, salads are much more than what is imprinted in our collective imagination. A dish dedicated to those who follow a restrictive diet or, even worse, to a gastronomic punishment. But that's not exactly the case.

Fruit, meats, fish, cereals, cheeses, and much more can be the real protagonists of greedy, rich, and colorful salads, capable of giving a quick lunch or dinner, without sacrificing taste. The concept of salad is not just about mixing different raw vegetables with a dressing. If we think of the bowls (in which all kinds of salads are served, we think for example of the Hawaiian Pokè) that we now find in many places or of Asian cuisine, we can say that the concept of salad takes on a very different meaning to what we have described above.

From raw fish to raw or cooked vegetables (grilled or boiled), to meats and the best cheeses, but also potatoes, legumes, aromatic herbs, fruit, and much more: these are the ingredients with which it is possible to compose our salad. Do not forget also the choice of the dressing which, even in this case, is not necessarily based on extra virgin olive oil, salt, and vinegar as is mainly the case in Mediterranean countries, where olives are grown and it is an ancient custom to use oil. produced by their milling. There are infinite types of dressings that have a creamy base: from yogurt to mustard or mayonnaise. One of the most famous is the French dressing, prepared with vinegar, French mustard (Dijon mustard, with a strong taste), extra virgin olive oil, and spices to taste. There are many types of dressing on the market, such as the one with aromatic herbs or the simple yogurt sauce.

Leaving creativity aside, there are some salads whose recipes are now codified and which have made the history of international gastronomy. Classics are easily offered in many international restaurants, easily replicable even at home.

Recipes

Pineapple Walnut Salad

Time required:
15 minutes

Servings: 04

INGREDIENTS

1 can pineapple chunks (20 ounces), properly drained
2 cups celery, sliced
1/2 cup walnuts, roughly chopped
1 to 2 tablespoons mayonnaise (or to taste) to moisten
1 tablespoon lemon juice, freshly squeezed to taste with salt
Leaves of lettuce

STEPS FOR COOKING

1. Combine the drained pineapple chunks, celery, and walnuts in a mixing dish.
2. Allow cooling completely.
3. Add enough mayonnaise to moisten, along with the lemon juice and a pinch of salt, to taste, just before serving.
4. Toss the pineapple salad ingredients together gently to combine.
5. Serve on a bed of mixed salad greens or lettuce leaves.

South Fruit Bowl

Time required:
10 minutes

Servings: 02

INGREDIENTS

1 C. buttermilk
1 (3 oz.) packages
instant vanilla
pudding
1 (8 oz.) cartons
Cool Whip
1 (11 oz.) cans
mandarin oranges,
drained
1 (11 oz.) cans
crushed pineapple,
drained
14 chocolate
cookies, crushed

STEPS FOR COOKING

1. In a bowl, add the pudding and buttermilk and mix until well combined.
2. Gently, fold in the whipped cream.
3. Add the remaining ingredients and gently, stir to combine.
4. Refrigerate to chill completely.
5. Enjoy chilled.

Fruit Salad Levantine

Time required:
3 hours

Servings: 08

INGREDIENTS

2 C. strawberries,
washed, hulled and
halved
1 large cantaloupe,
balled
1 large honeydew
melon, balled
1 1/2 tbsp white
sugar
1 lime, juice Dip
2 1/2 C. Greek
yogurt
1/4 C. whipping
cream
1/4 C. white sugar
2 tbsp orange juice
1/2 tsp orange rind
1/4 C. dates,
chopped
1/8 C. pistachios

STEPS FOR COOKING

1. For the salad: in a bowl, add all the ingredients and toss to coat well.
2. Cover the bowl and keep aside for about 30 minutes.
3. Now, place in the fridge to chill completely.
4. In another bowl, add the dates, whipping cream, yogurt, white sugar, orange rind and orange juice and mix until well combined.
5. Refrigerate to chill for about 3 hours.
6. Divide the salad onto serving plates and top with the dip.
7. Enjoy with a garnishing of the pistachios.

Easy Greek Salad

Time required:
15 minutes

Servings: 04

INGREDIENTS

1 teaspoon Black pepper,
1 teaspoon Sea salt,
1/3 cup Mint leaves, fresh chopped,
1/3 cup Kalamata olives,
1/3 cup Red onion, sliced thinly
5 ounces Feta cheese, cut into one-half inch cubes
2 cups Cherry tomatoes cut into halves,
1 Green bell pepper, chopped,
1 Cucumber, chopped
1/4 teaspoon Dijon mustard,

STEPS FOR COOKING

1. Blend together the garlic, oregano, salt, mustard, black pepper, vinegar, and olive oil.

2. On a large serving platter, arrange the cherry tomatoes, cucumber, red onions, olives, green pepper, and feta cheese attractively.

3. Slowly pour the dressing over the veggies and gently toss all of the veggies around until they are well coated.

4. Then sprinkle the oregano and mint leaves on the top and season with the pepper and salt.

INGREDIENTS

1/2 teaspoon Oregano, dried,
1 tablespoon Garlic, minced,
3 tablespoons Red wine vinegar,
1/4 cup Extra virgin olive oil

STEPS FOR COOKING

Lebanese Taboule 'Salad

Time required:
25 minutes

Servings: 04

INGREDIENTS

60g fine bulgur
300g flat leaf
parsley
3 sprigs of mint
2 red onions
1 ½ lemons
100ml virgin olive oil
½ teaspoon
cinnamon
salt, pepper

STEPS FOR COOKING

1. The mint leaves and parsley must be plucked and finely chopped.
2. While we let the bulgur rise in warm water for 5 minutes, we can cut the tomato into small cubes and the onion into rings.
3. Now we can mix everything together and refine the taste with lemon juice, cinnamon, salt and pepper.

Weekend Breakfast Salad

Time required:
15 minutes

Servings: 04

INGREDIENTS

½ cup Cucumber, chopped
½ cup Dill, chopped
1 cup Almonds, chopped
1 cup Quinoa, cooked and cooled
1 Large Avocado, cut thin
1 Large Tomato, cut in wedges
1 Lemon
10 cups Arugula
2 tbsp. Olive oil
4 Eggs, hard- boiled

STEPS FOR COOKING

1. Mix together the quinoa, cucumber, tomatoes, and arugula.
2. Toss these ingredients lightly with olive oil, salt, and pepper.
3. Split the salad into 4 plates and position the egg and avocado on top.
4. Top each salad with almonds and herbs. Sprinkle with juice from the lemon.

Cherry & Apple Bowl

Time required:
25 minutes

Servings: 02

INGREDIENTS

1½ cups almond milk
½ cup pumpkin
puree
2 tablespoon
organic honey
2 tablespoon
almond butter
1 teaspoon organic
vanilla flavor
1 scoop Protein
powder
1 teaspoon ground
cinnamon
1/8 teaspoon
ground ginger
1/8 teaspoon cloves
¼ teaspoon ground
nutmeg
Pinch of salt
¼ cup chia seeds

STEPS FOR COOKING

1. In a blender, add all ingredients
   except chia seeds and pulse till
   smooth.
2. Transfer the amalgamation in a large
   bowl. Add chia seeds and stir to blend
   well.
3. Refrigerate for overnight.

Barley Breakfast Bowl with Lemon Yogurt Sauce

Time required:
10 minutes

Servings: 02

INGREDIENTS

¼ c. cut almonds, toasted

¼ c. fresh mint or parsley, chopped

¼ tsp. fresh ground black pepper

¼ tsp. kosher salt

½ tsp. Sea salt

1 c. Greek plain yogurt

1 c. mung bean sprouts (or preferred variety)

1 small avocado – peeled/pitted, and flesh diced or cut

1 tsp. Fresh lemon juice

STEPS FOR COOKING

1. First, prepare the Lemon Yogurt Sauce:

2. Mix the plain yogurt, lemon zest and juice, fresh mint or parsley, and salt & pepper in a container and stir to combine well.

3. Cover and place in your fridge until ready to serve.

4. After this, prepare the barley container: In a small mixing container, mix the barley, bean sprouts, cheese, almonds, and salt. Stir to mix thoroughly.

5. Split barley mixture into 2 serving bowls. Top each barley container with 2 tbsp. lemon yogurt sauce and avocado.

INGREDIENTS	STEPS FOR COOKING
1 tsp. lemon zest, finely grated 1/3 c. Cotija cheese or queso fresco - crumbled 1½ c. cooked barley, keep warm Fresh ground black pepper, to taste Lemon Yogurt Sauce Sea salt, to taste	6. Place a pinch of salt and pepper to taste, serve, and enjoy!

Balsamic Salmon Spinach Salad

Time required:
10 minutes

Servings: 04

INGREDIENTS

2 salmon fillets (6 ounces each)

6 cups fresh baby spinach

2 tbsps. chopped walnuts

2 tbsps. dried cranberries

4 tbsps. balsamic vinaigrette, divided

½ cup cubed avocado

2 tbsps. sunflower kernels Olive oil cooking spray

STEPS FOR COOKING

1. Spray a broiler pan with some cooking spray.

2. Place salmon in the pan. Trickle half the vinaigrette over the salmon.

3. Set up your oven to broil mode. Place the rack about 4 inches away from the heating element and preheat the oven.

4. Place the broiler pan in the oven and broil for 10 to 14 minutes or until cooked through.

5. Cut each salmon into two equal portions.

6. Place spinach in a large bowl. Drizzle remaining vinaigrette over it. Toss well.

7. Take four plates and divide equally the spinach among the plates.

INGREDIENTS	STEPS FOR COOKING
	8. Place a piece of salmon on each plate. Scatter avocado, sunflower kernels, walnuts and cranberries on top and serve.

Moroccan Salad

Time required:
10 minutes

Servings: 10

INGREDIENTS

¼ cup lemon juice

¼ teaspoon ground cinnamon

½ cup chopped fresh mint

½ cup extra-virgin olive oil

1 15-ounce can chickpeas, rinsed

1 cup finely diced carrot

1 small clove garlic, peeled and minced

1 teaspoon kosher salt, divided

1½ cups chopped fresh parsley

2 15-ounce cans dark red kidney beans, rinsed

STEPS FOR COOKING

1. In a salad bowl, whisk well lemon juice, cinnamon, olive oil, garlic, salt, parsley, and cumin.

2. Stir in remaining ingredients and toss well to coat in the dressing.

3. Serve and enjoy.

INGREDIENTS

*2 tablespoons
ground cumin*

*2 tablespoons
chopped fresh dill or
mint*

*3 cloves garlic,
pressed or minced*

*Small pinch red
pepper flakes*

STEPS FOR COOKING

Yogurt Cheese and Fruit

Time required:
15 minutes

Servings: 06

INGREDIENTS

¼ cup dried
cranberries or
raisins
¼ cup honey
½ cup orange juice
½ cup water
1 fresh Golden
Delicious apple
1 fresh pear
1 teaspoon fresh
lemon juice
3 cups plain nonfat
yogurt

STEPS FOR COOKING

1. Prepare the yogurt cheese the day before by lining a colander or strainer with cheesecloth.

2. Scoop the yogurt into the cheesecloth, put the strainer over a pot or container to catch the whey, and place in your fridge for minimum 8 hours before you serve. In a huge mixing container, combine the juices and water.

3. Chop the apple then pear into wedges, put the wedges in the juice mixture, allow it to sit for minimum five minutes.

4. Strain off the liquid. When the yogurt is firm, remove from fridge, slice, and place on plates.

5. Position the fruit wedges around the yogurt.

INGREDIENTS	STEPS FOR COOKING
	6. Sprinkle with honey and drizzle with cranberries or raisins just before you serve.

Pineapple Ambrosia

Time required:
45 minutes

Servings: 04

INGREDIENTS

1/2 cup
Coconut,
unsweetened
shredded,
1/2 cup
Pineapple, fresh
chopped,
1/2 cup Grapes
2 teaspoons Orange
zest,
1 cup Strawberries,
sliced,
1 tablespoon
Cornstarch,
1 cup Apples, fresh
sliced,
1/3 cup
Lemon juice
1/2 cup Tofu, soft,
pureed,

STEPS FOR COOKING

1. Mix the fruits all together in a larger mixing bowl and then set the bowl in the refrigerator to keep the fruits chilled.

2. Put the lemon juice and the cornstarch together in a small saucepot, then stir in the orange juice and simmer the mixture for ten minutes, constantly stirring until the mix begins to get thick.

3. When the mix is thick, then blend it together with the pureed tofu and then pour this over the fruit and toss gently, then serve.

INGREDIENTS

3 tablespoons
Orange juice,
1 cup Orange slices,

STEPS FOR COOKING

Nutty and Fruity Garden Salad

Time required:
10 minutes

Servings: 02

INGREDIENTS

6 cups baby spinach

½ cup chopped walnuts, toasted

1 ripe red pear, sliced

1 ripe persimmon, sliced

1 teaspoon garlic minced

1 shallot, minced

1 tablespoon extra-virgin olive oil

2 tablespoons fresh lemon juice

1 teaspoon whole-grain mustard

STEPS FOR COOKING

1. Mix well garlic, shallot, oil, lemon juice and mustard in a large salad bowl.
2. Add spinach, pear and persimmon. Toss to coat well.
3. To serve, garnish with chopped pecans.

Broccoli Salad with Sherry Vinaigrette

Time required:
25 minutes

Servings: 02

INGREDIENTS

2 cups broccoli
florets

⅓ cup extra-virgin
olive oil

½ Tbsp. sherry
vinegar

1 tsp. fresh thyme

½ tsp. Dijon mustard

½ cup green onion,
sliced

½ cup pecorino
cheese, shredded

¼ cup pecans,
toasted and
chopped Seasoning

STEPS FOR COOKING

1. Steam the broccoli until softened.
2. Ice bath the broccoli to cool, about 2 mins. Drain well dry with a tea towel.
3. In a large bowl, whisk oil, vinegar, thyme, mustard, and seasoning.
4. Add onion, broccoli, pecorino, and pecans, toss to combine, and serve.

Cobb Salad

Time required:
20 minutes

Servings: 04

INGREDIENTS

Vinaigrette
1/2 teaspoon Sea salt,
1/3 cup Balsamic vinegar,
1/2 cup Extra virgin olive oil,
1 tablespoon Dijon mustard,
1 teaspoon Garlic, minced,
1/2 teaspoon Black pepper,
6 cups Red chicory, chopped,
6 cups Kale, chopped,
2 Avocados, sliced
2 Chickpeas, drained and rinsed

STEPS FOR COOKING

1. Blend all of the listed ingredients for the salad dressing and then set it in the refrigerator until the salad is ready to serve.

2. Cook the tempeh bacon by the directions on the packaging. Set out four salad serving plates and divide the kale and red chicory evenly among the four plates.

3. Evenly divide the tomatoes, cucumber, corn, tempeh bacon, carrots, red onion, and chickpeas over the leafy salad on the serving plates.

4. Put the slices of avocado over the plates and then top with the chilled dressing.

Tempeh bacon
1/2 cup Red onion,
chopped,
1 cup Grape
tomatoes cut in half,
1 Cucumber peeled
and chopped
1/2 cup Corn,
thawed frozen or
fresh,
1 cup Carrots,
grated,

Goat Cheese Salad

Time required:
15 minutes

Servings: 04

INGREDIENTS

½ cup of walnuts
½ head of escarole (medium), torn
1 bunch of trimmed and torn arugula
1/3 cup extra virgin olive oil
2 bunches of medium beets (~1 ½ lbs.) with trimmed tops
2 tbsp. of red wine vinegar
4 oz. crumbled of goat cheese (aged cheese is preferred)
Kosher salt + freshly ground black pepper

STEPS FOR COOKING

1. Place the beets in water in a deep cooking pan and apply salt as seasoning.

2. Now, boil them using high heat for approximately twenty minutes or until they're soft. Peel them off when they're cool using your fingers or use a knife.

3. To taste, whisk the vinegar with salt and pepper in a big container. Then mix in the olive oil for the dressing.

4. Toss the beets with the dressing, so they're uniformly coated and marinate them for approximately fifteen minutes – 2 hours. Set the oven to 350F.

5. Bring the nuts on a baking sheet and toast them for approximately 8

INGREDIENTS	STEPS FOR COOKING

minutes (stirring them once) until they turn golden brown. Let them cool.

6. Mix and toss the escarole and arugula with the beets and put them in four plates.

7. Put in the walnuts and goat cheese as toppings before you serve. Enjoy

Tomato Salad

Time required:
25 minutes

Servings: 06

INGREDIENTS

1/4 cup Extra virgin olive oil,
1 pint Grape tomatoes, halved
1/4 cup Parsley, chopped fresh,
2 tablespoons Balsamic vinegar,
1 cup Yellow tomatoes, sliced thin,
1 Red onion, sliced thinly
1/2 teaspoon Sea salt,
1 cupRed tomatoes, sliced thin,
1 teaspoon Black pepper,
2 tablespoons Capers,

STEPS FOR COOKING

1. Blend the salt, pepper, olive oil, and vinegar in a medium-size mixing bowl until everything is well mixed together.

2. Toss the tomatoes and onions into this liquid mix and gently toss all of the veggies to coat them with the dressing mix.

3. Sprinkle the parsley and capers over the salad and serve.

Edamame & Asparagus Salad

Time required:
15 minutes

Servings: 02

INGREDIENTS

1 cup salad green, mixed

½ cup edamame, shelled and thawed

3 asparagus, end trimmed

2 Tbsp. apple cider vinegar

½ Tbsp. fresh cilantro, chopped

1 tsp. extra-virgin olive oil Seasoning

STEPS FOR COOKING

1. Preheat the grill to medium-high.
2. Grill the asparagus till slightly charred.
3. Place the greens, edamame, and asparagus on a large plate.
4. Whisk seasoning, oil, vinegar, and cilantro in a small bowl; and dress the salad.

Kauai Fruit Salad

Time required:
2 Hours

Servings: 08

INGREDIENTS

Salad
1 pineapple, cubed
*1 medium
cantaloupe cubed*
*1 medium honeydew
melon cubed*
*1 papaya, pared and
sliced*
*1 C. green grape,
halved lengthwise*
*1 C. strawberry,
halved lengthwise*
Dressing
*2 ripe bananas,
peeled, sliced*
1 C. sour cream
*1/4 C. firmly packed
brown sugar*
1 1/2 tsp lemon juice

STEPS FOR COOKING

1. For the dressing: in a food processor, add all the ingredients and pulse until smooth.

2. Transfer the dressing into a bowl and place in the fridge for about 3 hours.

3. In a bowl, place all the fruits and mix.

4. Divide the salad onto serving plates evenly.

5. Enjoy with a topping of the dressing.

Frozen Fruit Salad

Time required:
15 minutes

Servings: 08

INGREDIENTS	STEPS FOR COOKING

INGREDIENTS

½ cup whipping cream

2 (3-ounce) cream cheese packets (softened)

1 tablespoon mayonnaise

1/2 cup red maraschino cherries

1/2 cup maraschino cherries, green (quartered)

1 fruit cocktail (16- or 20-ounce) may (drained)

2 1/2 cups graham crackers (diced, about 24 marshmallows)

STEPS FOR COOKING

1. Collect the necessary Ingredient.
2. Using an electric mixer, whip the chilled heavy cream to firm peaks in a small mixing basin.
3. Cream the cream cheese and mayonnaise together in a large mixing dish using an electric mixer.
4. Fold in the whipped cream, cherries, fruit cocktail that has been drained, and marshmallows.
5. Fill a 1-quart freezer container or a loaf pan halfway with the ingredients.
6. Add more maraschino cherries or pecan halves as a garnish.
7. The salad should be frozen until it is firm. Then, remove the container from the oven and slice it to serve.

Gold Mango Fruit Salad

Time required:
30 minutes

Servings: 04

INGREDIENTS	STEPS FOR COOKING

INGREDIENTS

3 apricots, pitted and sliced

1 C. strawberry, quartered

1 C. kiwi, peeled, sliced

1 C. pineapple, chunks

1 banana, sliced

1 C. mango, peeled, chunked

Dressing

1/4 C. coconut milk

1 tbsp orange juice

1 tbsp honey

3 tbsp coconut, shredded

STEPS FOR COOKING

1. In a bowl, add all the fruit except banana and toss to coat.
2. Refrigerate for 2 hours.
3. Meanwhile, for the dressing: in a bowl, add all the ingredients and beat until well combined.
4. In the bowl of the fruit, add the dressing and banana and gently toss to coat.
5. Enjoy.

Grated Carrot Salad with Lemon-Dijon Vinaigrette

Time required:
25 minutes

Servings: 08

INGREDIENTS

9 small carrots (14 cm), peeled
2 tbsp.
1/2 teaspoon Dijon mustard
1 C. lemon juice
2 tbsp. extra virgin olive oil
1-2 tsp. honey (to taste)
¼ tsp. salt
¼ tsp. freshly ground pepper (to taste)
2 tbsp. chopped parsley
1 green onion, thinly sliced

STEPS FOR COOKING

1. First, grate the carrots in a food processor.
2. In a salad bowl, mix Dijon mustard, lemon juice, honey, olive oil, salt, and pepper.
3. Add the carrots, fresh parsley, and green onions.
4. Stir to coat well. Then Cover and refrigerate until ready to be serve.

Potato Salad with Herring

Time required:
25 minutes

Servings: 02

INGREDIENTS

400 g of firm-fleshed potatoes
1 small beet
2 shallots
150 g sweet smoked herring fillets
4 mixed oil
2 tablespoons vinegar
1 teaspoon of mustard
2 teaspoons chopped dill (fresh or frozen) Salt pepper

STEPS FOR COOKING

1. Wash the potatoes under running water, peel them, slice them and steam them for 20 minutes.

2. Cut the herring into cubes.

3. Peel the beetroot and cut into cubes. Peel and slice the shallots.

4. Mix mustard, oil, vinegar, and shallots.

5. Divide the still-warm potatoes and beet into 4 serving plates: salt very lightly and pepper. Add herring and vinaigrette, sprinkle with dill. Taste immediately.

Mayo-Less Tuna Salad

Time required:
30 minutes

Servings: 02

INGREDIENTS

5 oz. Tuna
1 tbsp. Olive oil
1 tbsp. Red wine
vinegar
¼ c. Chopped green
onion
2 c. Arugula
1 c. Cooked pasta
1 tbsp. Parmesan
cheese
Black pepper

STEPS FOR COOKING

1. Combine all ingredients into a
   medium bowl.
2. Split mixture between two plates.
3. Serve, and enjoy.

Shell Bean Salad

Time required:
45 minutes

Servings: 04

INGREDIENTS

150 g of shelling beans

30 g pasta, farfalle type

150 g fresh green beans

200 g tomatoes

1 carrot

1 bouquet garni

4 tablespoons olive oil

2 tablespoons balsamic vinegar

1/2 teaspoon of mustard

1 shallot

2 teaspoons chopped parsley

1 teaspoon chopped basil

Salt pepper

STEPS FOR COOKING

1. Shell the beans. Position them in a large saucepan and cover them completely with cold water. Add the bouquet garni, cover the pan. Let it simmer for 35 minutes.

2. Wash the green beans and mop them up. Cut in half, salt, and steam for 15 minutes.

3. Cook the pasta the time indicated on the package.

4. Peel and chop the shallot.

5. Prepare the vinaigrette with oil, vinegar, mustard, salt, and pepper. Add the shallot.

6. Wash tomatoes and carrot under running water. Rind off and grate the carrot, cut the tomatoes into wedges.

7. In a salad bowl, combine the shelling beans and the drained pasta, the green beans, the tomatoes, the carrot,

and the herbs. Add the vinaigrette and mix gently. Correct the seasoning if necessary.

Ambrosia

Time required:
2 hours 30
minutes

Servings: 08

INGREDIENTS

1 cup drained mixed fruit pieces or fruit cocktail
1/2 cup sectioned Mandarin oranges a
1/2 of pineapple tidbits
1/4 cup halved maraschino cherries
1/4 cup red grapes (seedless)
1/2 cup of small marshmallows
1/3 cup of sour cream, or as de-sired
1/4 cup flaked coconut (to use as a garnish)
6 lettuce leaves (or mixed greens

STEPS FOR COOKING

1. In a medium mixing basin, combine the drained fruits, marshmallows, sour cream, and coconut, stirring gently but thoroughly.

2. Refrigerate the fruit salad until it is completely cooled.

3. Salad should be served atop lettuce or mixed greens.

4. If you're feeding a large group or bring- in a bowl of ambrosia salad to a pot- luck, omit the lettuce and arrange fruit on top to form a pattern.

Rainbow Salmon Poke Bowl

Time required:
15 minutes

Servings: 02

INGREDIENTS

½ lb. salmon, diced

2 cups baby spinach

¼ cup cauliflower, riced

½ cup red cabbage, shredded

4 slices avocado

½ cup heart of palm, sliced

½ cup green onion, chopped

½ cup cilantro, chopped

1 Tbsp. lime juice

¼ cup coconut aminos

1 Tbsp. balsamic vinegar

2 Tbsp. extra-virgin avocado oil

STEPS FOR COOKING

1. Marinate for about 5 mins your diced salmon in avocado oil and lime juice.

2. Create a bed of spinach.

3. Add on top the riced cauliflower, diced salmon, cabbage, heart of palm, avocado slices.

4. Lightly, drizzle the spinach with your dressing of choice.

5. Dress your bowl with a splash of coconut aminos and balsamic vinegar, season to taste.

6. Garnish with a sprinkle of finely chopped green onion, cilantro, and chopped cashews.

INGREDIENTS

½ cup cashews, chopped

STEPS FOR COOKING

Trout Salad

Time required:
15 minutes

Servings: 02

INGREDIENTS	STEPS FOR COOKING
3 ½ tsp. extra-virgin olive oil	1. Drain and chop the anchovies.
1 ½ tsp. sesame oil	2. Simmer the trout fillet in water for approximately 10 mins (depending on the size) and set aside.
1 lemon peel, zest	
2 anchovies, canned in olive oil	3. Add chopped romaine heart, cucumber, parsley, and celery to a bowl and set aside.
1garlic clove, crushed	
½ lettuce romaine, chopped	4. In a bowl, whisk olive oil, sesame oil, tahini, crushed garlic, apple cider vinegar, orange zest, chopped anchovies, and black pepper.
½ fresh parsley, chopped bunch	
2 stalks celery	5. Top the salad with rainbow trout, drizzle dressing over, and finish with a hemp seeds sprinkle.
5 oz. rainbow trout, fillets	
2 ½ Tbsp. hemp seeds, shelled 1 Tbsp. apple cider vinegar	
1 ½ Tbsp. tahini Seasoning	

Kiwi Salad Kingston

Time required:
60 minutes

Servings: 12

INGREDIENTS

1/2 C. sugar

1/2 C. water

1/2 C. basil leaves, packed

1 tbsp lime rind, grated

4 C. pineapple, cubed

3 C. strawberries, quartered

4 kiwi, peeled and sliced

2 C. mangoes, peeled and cubed

STEPS FOR COOKING

1. For the simple syrup: in a pot, add the sugar and water and cook until boiling.

2. Cook for about 1 minute, stirring continuously.

3. Remove from the heat and stir in the lime rind and basil.

4. Remove from the heat and keep aside to cool.

5. Through a strainer, strain the mixture, discarding the solids.

6. In a bowl, add the fruits and syrup and gently, toss to coat well.

7. Enjoy.

Turkey Broccoli Salad

Time required:
10 minutes

Servings: 04

INGREDIENTS

*8 cups broccoli
florets
3 cooked skinless,
boneless chicken
breast halves, cubed
6 green onions,
chopped
1 cup mayonnaise
¼ cup apple cider
vinegar
¼ cup honey*

STEPS FOR COOKING

1. In a large bowl combine broccoli, chicken and green onions
2. After whisk mayonnaise, vinegar, and honey together in a bowl until well blended.
3. Then pour mayonnaise dressing over broccoli mixture and toss to coat.
4. After cover and refrigerate until chilled, if desired. Serve.

Carrot Sticks with Avocado Dip

Time required:
10 minutes

Servings: 06

INGREDIENTS	STEPS FOR COOKING
½ cup cilantro, firmly packed ½ onion 1 big avocado, pitted 1 tablespoon of chili-garlic sauce or chili sauce 2 tablespoon olive oil 6 ounces shelled edamame Juice of one lemon Salt and pepper	1. Put the edamame, cilantro, onion, and chili sauce in a blender or food processor. 2. Pulse it to cut and mix the ingredients. Put in the avocado and the lemon juice. 3. Slowly put in the olive oil as you blend. Move to a jar. 4. Scoop 2 spoons and serve with carrot sticks

Cranberry & Cauliflower Salad

Time required:
30 minutes

Servings: 02

INGREDIENTS

4 cups cauliflower
florets
4 Tbsp. extra-virgin
olive oil
½ cup cranberries
2 large eggs
¼ cup apple cider
vinegar
1 Tbsp. shallot,
minced
½ tsp. Dijon mustard
½garlic clove, grated
4 cups radicchio
⅓ cup pecans,
toasted and
chopped
¼ cup feta cheese,
crumbled Seasoning

STEPS FOR COOKING

1. Preheat the oven to 425°F.
2. Coat a baking sheet with parchment paper.
3. Toss the cauliflower with oil and seasoning in a large bowl.
4. Place it in the prepared baking sheet and roast until almost tender.
5. Add the cranberries and continue to roast for about 5 mins more.
6. Whisk remaining oil, vinegar, shallot, mustard, garlic, and seasoning in the bowl.
7. Meanwhile, place the eggs to boil: 5 mins for medium-soft yolks or 6 mins for medium-firm. Drain and cover with ice water. Then, when cool, peel and cut in half.
8. Add escarole and coat with the dressing. Add the eggs, roasted

INGREDIENTS	STEPS FOR COOKING
	vegetables, pecans, and feta cheese and toss to combine.
9. Serve the salad topped with the eggs quartered.

Lentil Salad

Time required:
10 minutes

Servings: 02

INGREDIENTS

½ cup parsley
1 red bell pepper
1 tbsp. lime juice
1 tbsp. olive oil
2 cups lentil
3 spring onions
A pinch of salt
15 basil leaves
Turmeric – to your taste

STEPS FOR COOKING

1. Cook the lentils based on the package instructions.
2. Put in a garlic clove while cooking. When cooled, remove the garlic clove and put the lentils into a big container.
3. Chop all the vegetables then put in them to the lentils.
4. Put in lime juice, a small amount of salt, and olive oil. Mix thoroughly.

Farro Salad with Arugula

Time required:
45 minutes

Servings: 02

INGREDIENTS

½ cup farro
½ teaspoon ground black pepper
½ teaspoon Italian seasoning
½ teaspoon olive oil1 ½ cup chicken stock
1 cucumber, chopped
1 tablespoon lemon juice
1 teaspoon salt
2 cups arugula, chopped

STEPS FOR COOKING

1. Mix up together farro, salt, and chicken stock and move mixture in the pan.
2. Close the lid and boil it for a little more than half an hour. In the meantime, place all rest of the ingredients in the salad container.
3. Chill the farro to the room temperature and put in it in the salad container too. Mix up the salad well.

Shoepeg Corn Salad

Time required:
10 minutes

Servings: 04

INGREDIENTS	STEPS FOR COOKING

INGREDIENTS

¼ cup Greek yogurt
½ cup cherry
tomatoes halved
1 cup shoepeg corn,
drained
1 jalapeno pepper,
chopped
1 tablespoon chives,
chopped
1 tablespoon lemon
juice
3 tablespoons fresh
cilantro, chopped

STEPS FOR COOKING

1. In the salad container, mix up together shoepeg corn, cherry tomatoes, jalapeno pepper, chives, and fresh cilantro.

2. Put in lemon juice and Greek yogurt. Mix yo the salad well.

3. Put in your fridge and store it for maximum 1 day

Chicken, Brussels Sprouts & Mushrooms Salad

Time required:
10 minutes

Servings: 02

INGREDIENTS

6 oz. chicken, shredded and cooked

2 cups fresh mushrooms

2 cups Brussels sprouts

2 cups baby arugula

½ cup celery

3 Tbsp. extra-virgin olive oil

1 ½ Tbsp. apple cider vinegar

1 Tbsp. shallot

½ Tbsp. Dijon mustard

1 tsp. fresh thyme

½ cup Pecorino cheese Seasoning

STEPS FOR COOKING

1. Shave the mushrooms and Brussel sprouts, slice the celery, and mince the shallot.

2. Whisk oil, vinegar, shallot, mustard, thyme, and pepper in a large bowl.

3. Add chicken, mushrooms, Brussels sprouts, arugula, and celery; toss to coat.

4. Serve with Pecorino cheese shards.

Quinoa Salad

Time required:
10 minutes

Servings: 02

INGREDIENTS

¼ tsp sea salt

½ cup quinoa
(uncooked)

1 carrot

1 tbsp. apple cider
vinegar

1 tbsp. flaxseed oil

2 brussels sprouts

STEPS FOR COOKING

1. Wash quinoa meticulously. Dice the carrots and brussels sprouts to minuscule pieces.

2. Cook the quinoa based on the instruction on the packaging.

3. Mix flaxseed oil, sea salt, and apple cider vinegar. Sauté brussels sprouts and carrots on a small amount of olive oil for a few minutes.

4. After both brussels sprouts and carrots, and quinoa are ready, combine them all in a container.

5. Put in the dressing and mix meticulously. Serve warm.

Avocado Pomegranate Dip

Time required:
5 minutes

Servings: 02

INGREDIENTS	STEPS FOR COOKING
3 medium avocados, diced 1 Tbsp. fresh cilantro, chopped ½ shallot finely, chopped ¼ tsp. cumin, grounded ½ Tbsp. jalapeño, finely chopped ⅔ medium pomegranate, seeded 2 Tbsp. lemon juice Seasoning	1. Slightly mash the avocado with a fork. 2. Gently mix all the ingredients adding the pomegranate seeds at the end.

Wheatberry Salad

Time required:
60 minutes

Servings: 02

INGREDIENTS

¼ cup fresh parsley, chopped

¼ cup of wheat berries

1 cup of water

1 tablespoon canola oil

1 tablespoon chives, chopped

1 teaspoon chili flakes

1 teaspoon salt

2 oz. pomegranate seeds

2 tablespoons walnuts, chopped

STEPS FOR COOKING

1. Put wheat berries and water in the pan.

2. Put in salt and simmer the ingredients for about fifty minutes over the moderate heat.

3. In the meantime, mix up together walnuts, chives, parsley, pomegranate seeds, and chili flakes.

4. When the wheatberry is cooked, move it in the walnut mixture.

5. Put in canola oil and mix up the salad well.

Strawberry Poppy Seed Dressing

Time required:
10 minutes

Servings: 04

INGREDIENTS

¼ cup of raspberry vinegar

¼ tsp of ground ginger

¼ tsp of sea salt

½ tsp of onion powder

½ tsp of poppy seeds

1/3 cup of extra-virgin olive oil

1/3 cup of honey

2 tbsp. of freshly squeezed orange juice

STEPS FOR COOKING

1. Put all ingredients, apart from the poppy seeds and oil into a blender.

2. Blend until the desired smoothness is achieved and creamy.

3. Next, progressively put the oil into the mixture until blended.

4. Put in in the poppy seeds and stir thoroughly. Put in a mason jar then place in your fridge before you serve.

5. Keep for maximum 3 days. Serve with your garden salads

6. Tomato and Mushroom Sauce.

Green Buddha Bowl

Time required:
15 minutes

Servings: 02

INGREDIENTS

1 tablespoon olive oil
1 lb brussels sprouts, trimmed and halved
Salt and black pepper, to taste
2 cups cooked quinoa
1 cup red apple, chopped
¼ cup pepitas
1 avocado, sliced
1 ½ cups arugula
½ cup of mayo
¾ cup plain Greek yogurt
1 teaspoon ground mustard
¼ cup Pompeian White Balsamic Vinegar

STEPS FOR COOKING

1. Mix quinoa with apple and the rest of the ingredients in a salad bowl.
2. Serve.
3. Serving Suggestion: Serve the bowl with spaghetti squash.
4. Variation Tip: Add some edamame beans to the bowl.

INGREDIENTS

STEPS FOR COOKING

½ teaspoon salt
1 tablespoon fresh
basil, chopped
1 garlic clove,
minced

Panzanella Salad

Time required:
15 minutes

Servings: 04

INGREDIENTS

2 cucumbers,
chopped
1 red onion, sliced
2 red bell peppers,
chopped
¼ cup fresh cilantro,
chopped
1 tablespoon capers
1 oz whole-grain
bread, chopped
1 tablespoon canola
oil
½ teaspoon minced
garlic
1 tablespoon Dijon
mustard
1 teaspoon olive oil
1 teaspoon lime
juice

STEPS FOR COOKING

1. Pour canola oil into the skillet and bring it to boil.

2. Add chopped bread and roast it until crunchy (3-5 minutes).

3. Meanwhile, in the salad bowl, combine sliced red onion, cucumbers, bell peppers, cilantro, capers, and mix up gently.

4. Make the dressing: mix up together lime juice, olive oil, Dijon mustard, and minced garlic.

5. Put the dressing over the salad and stir it directly before serving.

Peach & Jalapeno Dip

Time required:
15 minutes

Servings: 02

INGREDIENTS

3 lb. ripe peaches
1 jalapeño chili
½ Tbsp. oil
1 lemon
1 ½ cup water,
filtered
1 Tbsp. Stevia,
granulated
1 tsp. sea salt

STEPS FOR COOKING

1. Peel the lemon, making sure to omit any white bit, and juice the pulp.

2. Peel the peaches and discard the stone and coat them in sugar. Set aside for 20 mins.

3. In the meantime, seed and roughly chop the jalapeño.

4. In a medium saucepan, heat the oil and jalapeño until it softened. Add water if necessary.

5. Add the peaches, lemon peels, and juice, set to simmer for 20 mins.

6. Mash the fruit with a fork and remove the lemon peel.

Shrimp Salad

Time required:
45 minutes

Servings: 02

INGREDIENTS

2 tablespoons olive oil

1/3 cup red onion, chopped

3 cups broccoli slaw

3 cups broccoli florets

1/2 teaspoon salt

2 garlic cloves, minced

1/2 pound shrimp, peeled and deveined

1 teaspoon lime juice

Green onions, chopped, for garnish

Cilantro, chopped

Sriracha and red pepper flakes, for garnish

STEPS FOR COOKING

1. Mix all the sesame almond dressing in a bowl.

2. Saute onion with oil in a skillet for 5 minutes.

3. Stir in broccoli slaw and florest then saute for 7 minutes.

4. Add black pepper and salt then transfer to a plate.

5. Add minced garlic, shrimp, lime juice and more oil to the same skillet.

6. Saute for 5 minutes then transfer the shrimp to the broccoli.

7. Pour the sesame dressing on top and garnish with cilantro and green onions.

8. Serve warm.

Sesame almond dressing:
2 tablespoons almond butter
2 tablespoons water
1 tablespoon sesame oil
1 tablespoon tamari
1 tablespoon maple syrup
1 teaspoon lime juice
1 teaspoon ginger, minced
1 clove minced garlic
1 teaspoon sriracha sauce
1/4 teaspoon black pepper

Asian Slaw

Time required:
15 minutes

Servings: 04

INGREDIENTS

2 cups green cabbage, shredded
1/2 cup carrots, shredded
1/2 cup cilantro, chopped
1/2 cup bell peppers, sliced
1/2 cup peanuts, crushed Avocado slices
Dressing:
2 tablespoons peanut butter
1 teaspoon agave syrup
1 tablespoon soy sauce
1 teaspoon white wine vinegar

STEPS FOR COOKING

1. First, mix all the dressing ingredients in a salad bowl.
2. Stir in rest of the slaw ingredients and mix well.
3. Serve.

INGREDIENTS

1 teaspoon lime juice
1 tablespoon water
Salt and black black pepper to taste

STEPS FOR COOKING

Cambodian Fruit Salad

Time required:
25 minutes

Servings: 08

INGREDIENTS

Syrup:
3/4 C. coconut milk
2 tbsp sugar
1 tbsp chopped fresh lemongrass, chopped
Salad:
1 medium pineapple, peeled and cubed
1 mango, peeled and cubed
4 yellow kiwi fruits, peeled and cubed
2 bananas, peeled and sliced
1 grated lime, zest

STEPS FOR COOKING

1. For the syrup: in a pot, add all the ingredients and cook until boiling.
2. Cook for about 2 minutes, stirring continuously.
3. Remove from the heat and through a strainer, strain the syrup into a bowl.
4. Place in the fridge for about 40 minutes.
5. For the salad: in a bowl, add all the ingredients and mix well.
6. Pour the syrup over salad and gently, toss to coat.
7. Enjoy.

Frozen Pineapple-Cranberry Salad

Time required:
20 minutes

Servings: 12

INGREDIENTS

One can crushed pineapple (20 oz) (well-drained)

2 cans full cranberry sauce (14 oz.) sour cream (16 oz.)

2cups whipped topping (frozen) (thawed or prepared Dream Whip)

½ cup of confectioner's sugar

1/2 cup walnuts or pecans (coarsely chopped)

STEPS FOR COOKING

1. Collect the necessary Ingredient.
2. Grease a 9 x 13 x 2-inch baking dish lightly.
3. Combine the pineapple, cranberry sauce, sour cream, whipped topping, confectioners' sugar, and nuts if used in a large mixing bowl.
4. Fill the baking dish halfway with the fruit mixture.
5. Freeze the fruit salad for several hours or overnight until it is completely firm.
6. Cut the frozen salad into squares and place on salad leaves to serve.
7. Serve and have fun!

Passion Fruit Vinaigrette

Time required:
10 minutes

Servings: 08

INGREDIENTS	STEPS FOR COOKING

2 passion fruits (or 1/4 cup puree from passion fruit)
1/2 cup extra virgin olive oil
a quarter-cup of lime juice
1teaspoon of vinegar 2 tablespoons honey
1/4 teaspoon salt

1. Collect the necessary Ingredient.
2. Passion fruits should be cut in half. Then, into a small saucepan, scrape the pulp and seeds.
3. Over medium-low heat, cook the fruit pulp, stirring often. Bring the pulp to a near-boiling point, then remove it from the heat.
4. Using a fine sieve or colander, strain the pulp.
5. Remove the seeds and set the liquid aside to cool.
6. In a blender or food processor, combine the passion fruit juice, olive oil, lime juice, vinegar, honey, and salt until smooth.
7. The salad dressing kept in the refrigerator for up to a week. Before using, give it a good stir or shake.

Savory Buckwheat Bowls

Time required:
30 minutes

Servings: 10

INGREDIENTS

1 cup Buckwheat groats, toasted
1 tablespoon Extra virgin olive oil
2 cups Water
Sea salt
.5Onion, diced
4 Button mushrooms, sliced – chopped
2 Eggs
1 tablespoon Capers.

STEPS FOR COOKING

1. Rinse and transfer the buckwheat along with the water and sea salt to a saucepan. Over medium heat, cook the buckwheat groats until the water has been absorbed and the groats are fluffy. Remove from the sun, cover with a lid, and sit for 10 minutes with the groats.

2. Meanwhile, add to the pan the extra virgin olive oil and onion, along with a tiny sprinkle of sea salt. Enable the onion to cook slowly over low heat until the caramelized onion is darkened, stirring regularly. Bring in the parsley and mushrooms and saute for five minutes until the mushrooms are tender.

3. In the skillet, add the cooked buckwheat, mix it and encourage the flavors to meld and cook together for an additional two minutes.

INGREDIENTS	STEPS FOR COOKING
	4. When your buckwheat finishes frying, prepare your eggs in a separate pan according to your choice. Cover the cooked eggs and capers with the buckwheat, then serve immediately.

Berries & Watermelon Salad

Time required:
20 minutes

Servings:08

INGREDIENTS

2½ pound seedless watermelon, cubed

2 cartons fresh strawberries, hulled and sliced

2 cups fresh blueberries

1 tablespoon fresh gingerroot, grated

¼-ounce fresh mint leaves, chopped

1 tablespoon raw honey

¼ cup fresh lime juice

STEPS FOR COOKING

1. In a sizable bowl, mix together all ingredients.
2. Serve immediately.

Lightning Source UK Ltd.
Milton Keynes UK
UKHW020924010721
386455UK00005B/40